More KinderClips

EARLY LEARNING PATTERNS

by Marilynn G. Barr

Publisher: Roberta Suid
Copy Editor: Annalisa Suid
Design and Production: Marilynn G. Barr
Educational Consultant: Sarah Felstiner

Monday Morning Books is a trademark of
Monday Morning Books, Inc.

Entire contents copyright © 1993
by Monday Morning Books, Inc., Box 1680, Palo Alto, California 94302

For a complete catalog, write to the address above.

ISBN 1-878279-60-2

Printed in the United States of America

9 8 7 6 5 4 3 2 1

Contents

Contents

Introduction

Welcome to a brand new collection of kinderclips!

We've divided the patterns in this book into three categories: **Let's Play**, **Around Town** and **Throughout the Year**. The first section, called **Let's Play**, has patterns that are close to real sizes: a mailbox, postcard forms, stamps, book plates, checks and play money, a telephone, and more. The patterns in **Let's Play** are useful for pre-writing activities. The clips in **Around Town** are miniatures. These paper-doll sized patterns allow children to build their own town, a city that they've visited, or one that exists in their minds only.

The California Social Studies Framework advises, "To develop geographic learnings, children need to build a three-dimensional floor or table map of their immediate geographic region. Such an activity helps develop children's observational skills, teaches the concepts of geographic scale, distance, and relative location; and clarifies for children the spatial relationships among the region's features. Small building blocks or milk cartons can be used to simulate neighborhood structures. Street signs, signals, crosswalks, mailboxes, and model vehicles, such as delivery trucks, dumpsters, cars, and buses, can be added to represent the variety of human activities going on in this region."

Don't feel limited to using the **Around Town** clips in this way, only. The patterns are perfect for spicing up bulletin boards, newsletters, calendars, worksheets, and more.

The **Throughout the Year** section includes stickers and display patterns for every month. Enlarge them for children to color or decorate with various crafts materials. Reduce the patterns, make duplicates, and glue onto cardboard squares to make Concentration games. Picture bingo can be made by gluing onto grids. There are weather clips for children to use in charting the weekly weather on a large classroom calendar, happy birthday clips to mark students' birthdays, a fire hat (for fire safety week), a clock (for daylight saving time), a globe for Earth Day, etc.

Most importantly, have fun with these adorable pictures! They lend themselves to fun, creative projects, so let your mind wander . . . and enjoy!

TEACHER PAGES

LET'S PLAY

The mailbox pattern in the post office section can be glued to the front of a shoe box for extra sturdiness. Let children write or draw on the letter forms and postcards. Stamps can be colored and then glued onto their letters. Turn the mailbox into a special Valentine mailbox, and let students use the postcards to send their friends Valentine messages. Or set up a permanent message center in your classroom. One teacher or parent volunteer should be in charge of this center, to assist children in delivering their letters, writing names on the envelopes, or reading messages written by other classmates.

The library patterns give students an opportunity to play-act the different experiences they have in a library. They can make their own book plates to glue in home-made books. Library cards allow them to practice writing their names.

TEACHER PAGES

LET'S PLAY

Playing school is a favorite game of many children. These patterns let them play with their own alphabet sets. Duplicate copies for each student to make into ABC books. The school bell and clock can be glued on heavy cardboard and covered with Contact paper for extra staying power.

The check forms and play money from the office section can also be used in a dramatic play store. Glue the very modern cordless telephone onto heavy cardboard and the computer pattern onto a shoe box.

TEACHER PAGES

AROUND TOWN

Children can build their own town or neighborhoods using the Around Town clips. Dwelling patterns can be glued onto cereal boxes, shoe boxes, and milk cartons. You might want to supplement the clips with photos of familiar places in your school's neighborhood. (These might also be glued onto boxes.)

Allow children plenty of space to build their town. They may want to work together to lay out the buildings in the appropriate places. Or each child might want to work on a neighborhood by himself or herself. Provide students with crayons, non-toxic markers, and other craft materials to decorate these patterns.

Many of the clips in this section can be used in a variety of ways. If a guest speaker has been invited to the classroom (a police officer, firefighter, principal, librarian, etc.), children can prepare for the meeting by play-acting with the drawings from those sections of Around Town. Or if the class is going on a field trip to a firehouse, you might set up a play table with the various firefighter clips.

IDEAS FOR USES OF INDIVIDUAL CLIPS

Movie theater screen: Children can draw their own picture on the blank screen. Or, take a polaroid of each child and glue each one to a separate screen. The border can be decorated by the student and used to designate his or her seat at an open house.

Library: Children can make their own library dioramas in shoe boxes and rehearse the rules of the library before going there as a class. Students can draw little books to go into their libraries, and even stage mini-story hours for each other.

Hospital/Doctor: Before children visit a doctor's office for check-ups, the class can use the doctor/hospital props to rehearse what a visit to the doctor's office is like. This may help remove some of the fear of visiting a doctor.

Bus: Reproduce the bus and enlarge to put on a bulletin board. Have children draw small self-portraits. Glue their faces into the windows. Draw your own picture for the bus driver's seat.

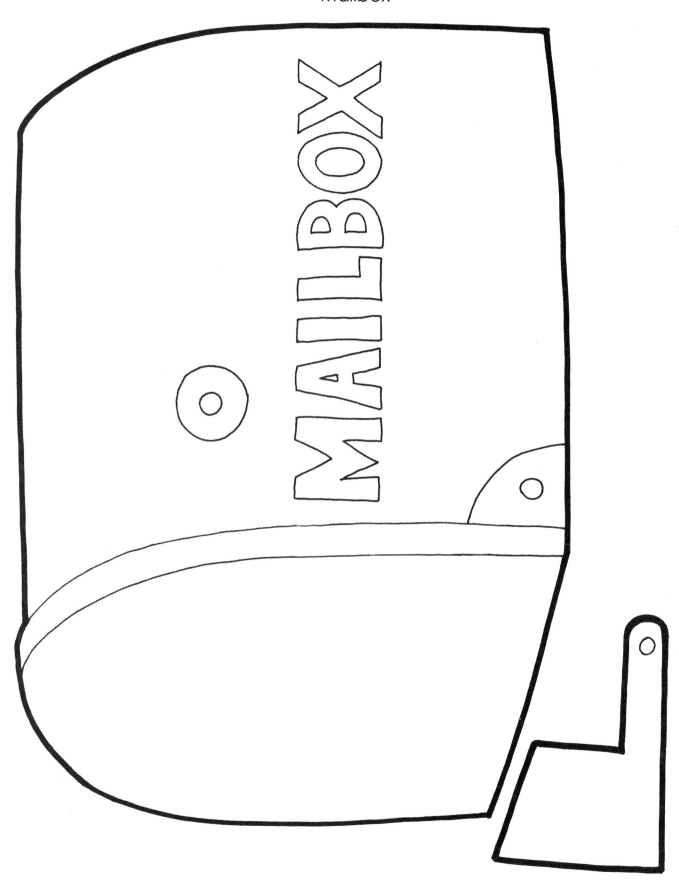

Let's Play Post Office
Letter Forms

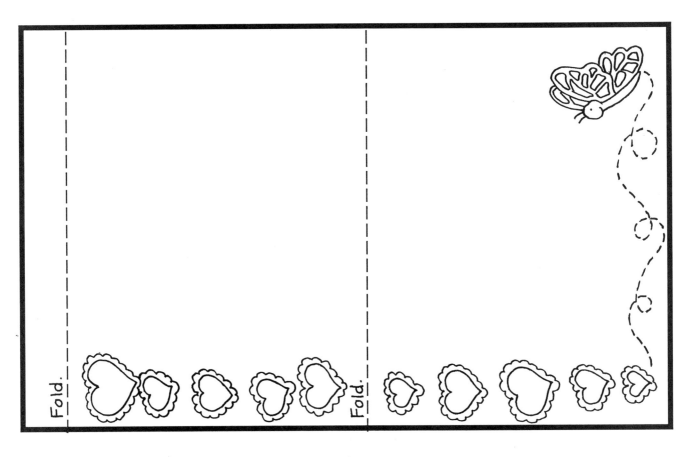

10

Let's Play Post Office
Postcard Forms

Let's Play Post Office
Stamps

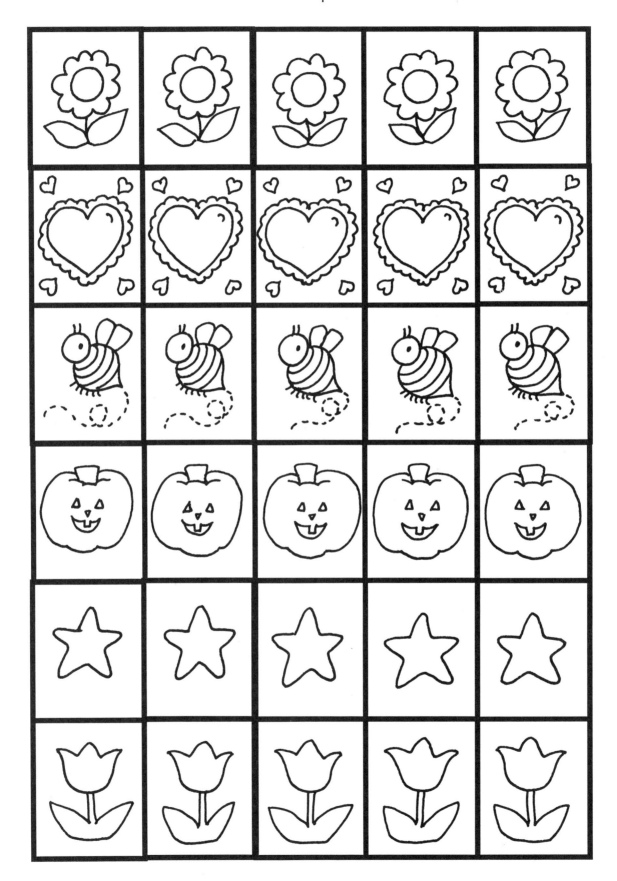

More KinderClips

Let's Play Library
Books

Let's Play Library
Book Plates

My Book

_____
Name

My Book

_____
Name

My Book

_____
Name

My Book

_____
Name

My Book

_____
Name

My Book

_____
Name

Let's Play Library
Library Cards

This Library Card belongs to

_____
Name

This Library Card belongs to

_____
Name

This Library Card belongs to

_____
Name

This Library Card belongs to

_____
Name

This Library Card belongs to

_____
Name

This Library Card belongs to

_____
Name

Let's Play Library
Due Date Cards

_____

Book Title

This book is due back in the library by _____, _____.
　　　day　　　　　date

_____
Signature

_____

Book Title

This book is due back in the library by _____, _____.
　　　day　　　　　date

_____
Signature

_____

Book Title

This book is due back in the library by _____, _____.
　　　day　　　　　date

_____
Signature

_____

Book Title

This book is due back in the library by _____, _____.
　　　day　　　　　date

_____
Signature

_____

Book Title

This book is due back in the library by _____, _____.
　　　day　　　　　date

_____
Signature

_____

Book Title

This book is due back in the library by _____, _____.
　　　day　　　　　date

_____
Signature

Let's Play School
Alphabet A-H

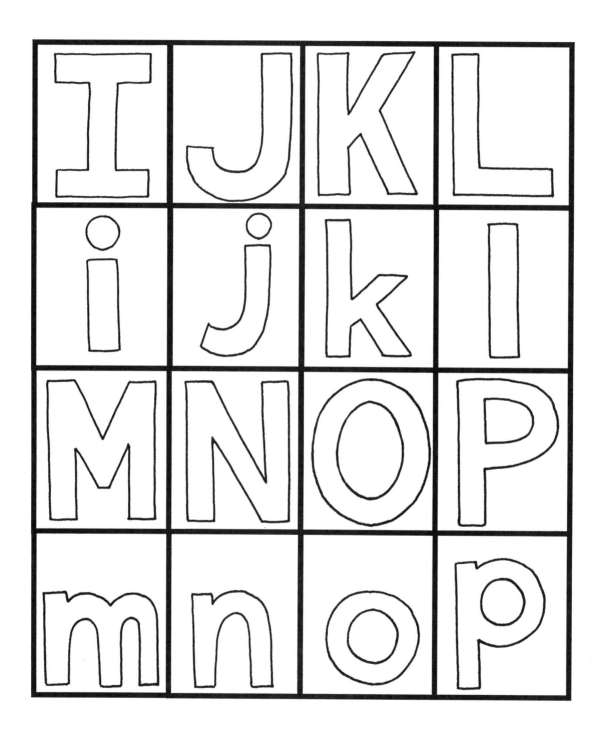

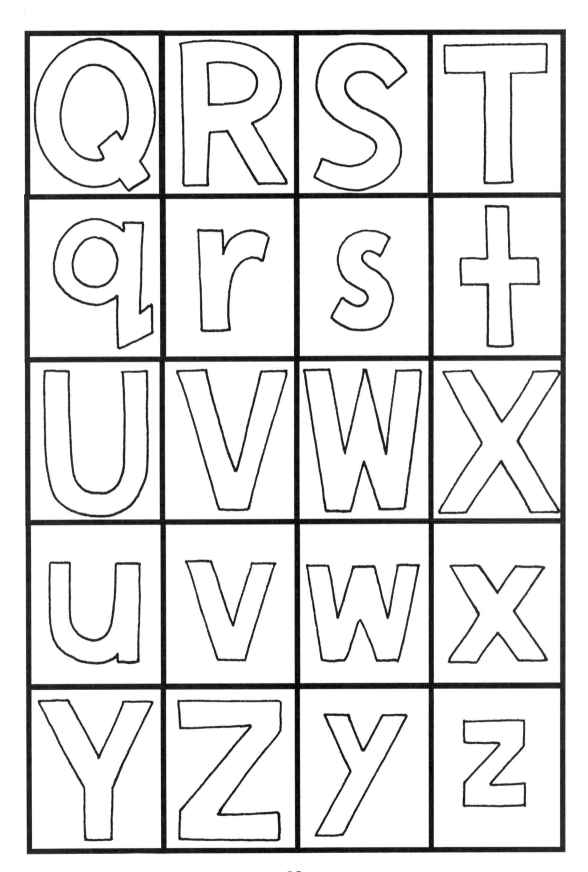

20

Let's Play School
Buddy Badges

We're Buddies
_____
Name

We're Buddies
_____
Name

We're Buddies
_____
Name

We're Buddies
_____
Name

We're Buddies
_____
Name

We're Buddies
_____
Name

More KinderClips

Let's Play School
School Bell & Clock

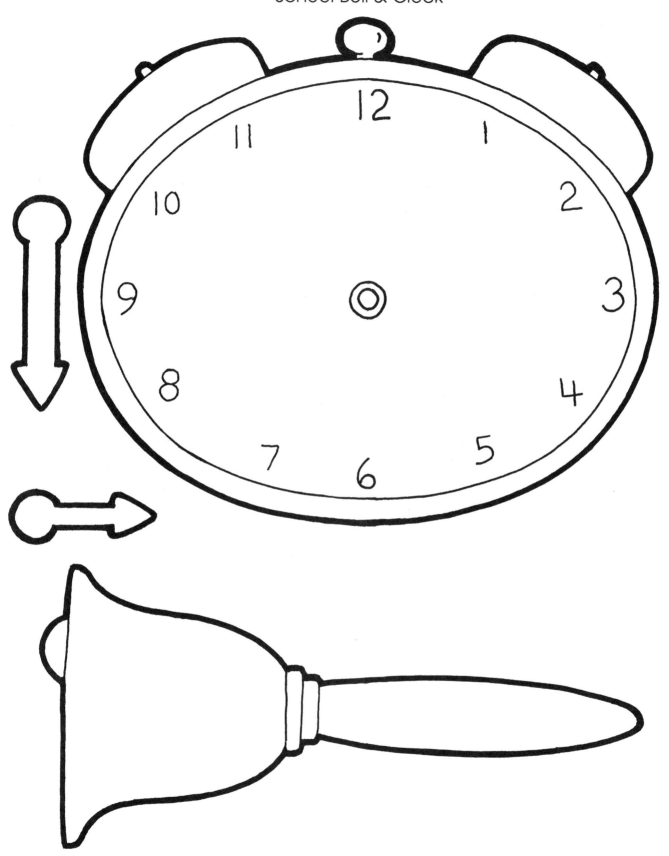

Let's Play Office
Check Forms and Play Money

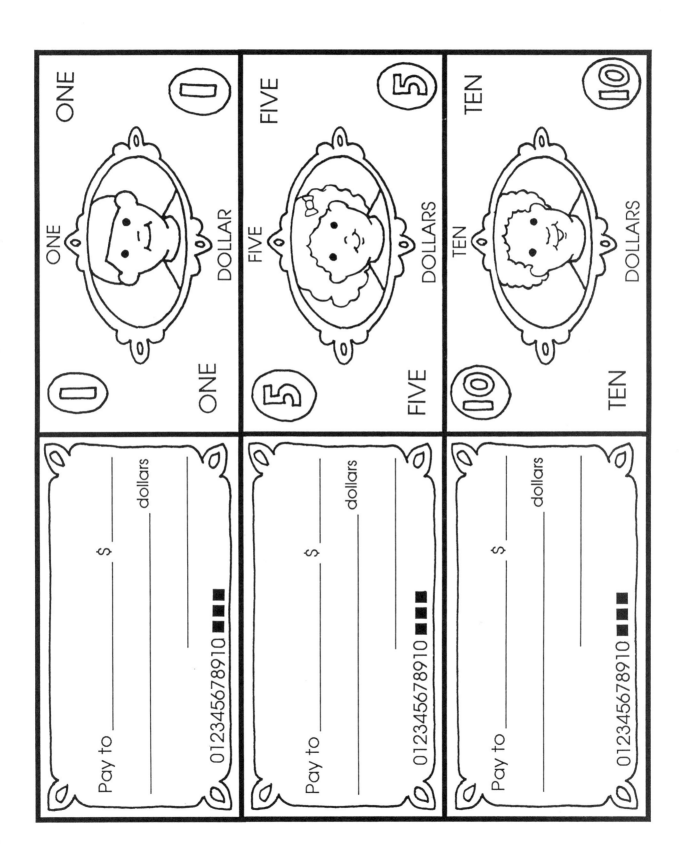

Let's Play Office
"While You Were Out" Message Forms

While You Were Out

_____
Caller's Name

For _____
Name

☐ Called and will call back

☐ Wants you to call back

☐ Left a message

Date _____

Time _____

While You Were Out

_____
Caller's Name

For _____
Name

☐ Called and will call back

☐ Wants you to call back

☐ Left a message

Date _____

Time _____

While You Were Out

_____
Caller's Name

For _____
Name

☐ Called and will call back

☐ Wants you to call back

☐ Left a message

Date _____

Time _____

While You Were Out

_____
Caller's Name

For _____
Name

☐ Called and will call back

☐ Wants you to call back

☐ Left a message

Date _____

Time _____

 More KinderClips

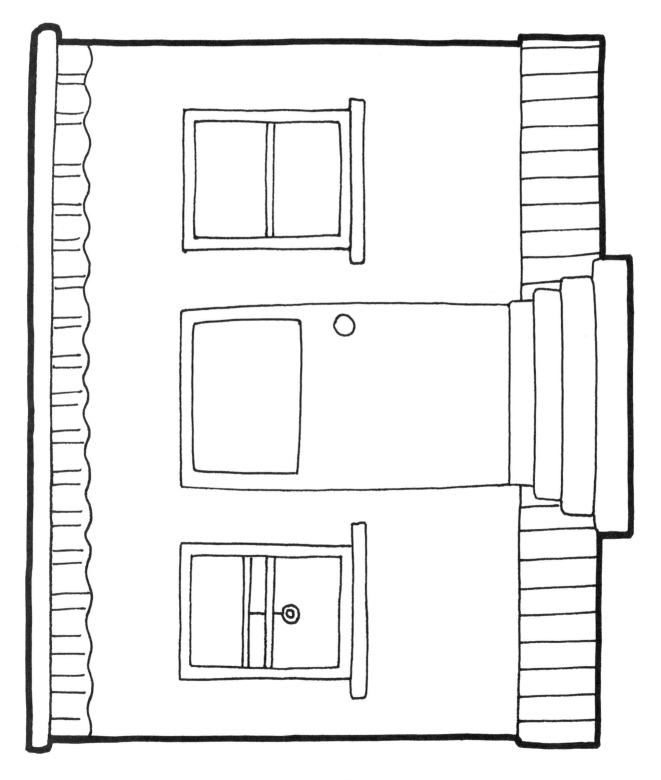

Around Town–People to Know
Caucasian Family

African American Family

More KinderClips

Around Town–People to Know
Asian Family

33

Around Town–People to Know
Hispanic Family

Around Town–People to Know
Native American Family

More KinderClips

36

Around Town–School
School Employees

Around Town–School
Flags

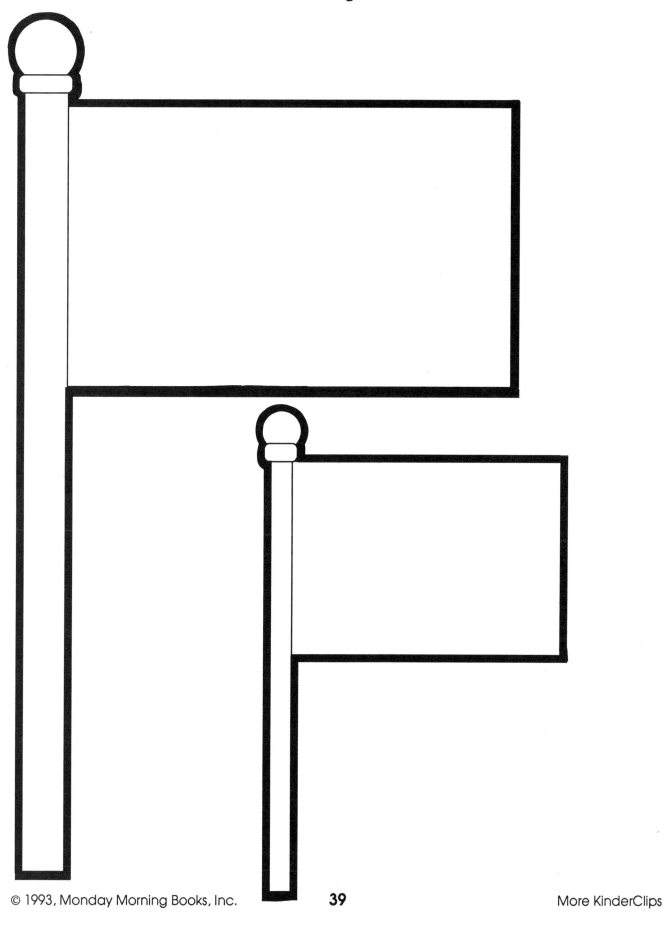

Around Town–Library
Librarian and Library Supplies

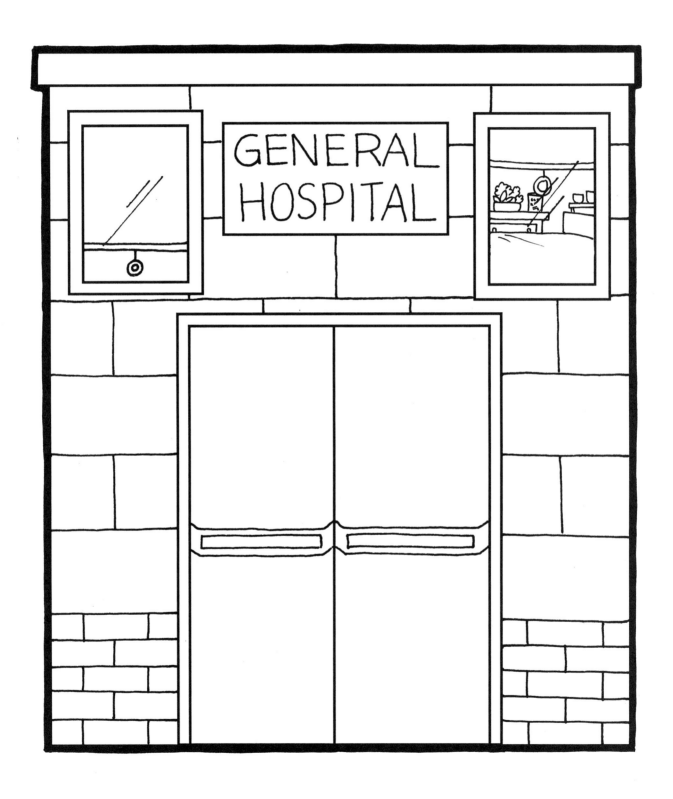

42

More KinderClips

Around Town–Hospital

Hospital Employees and Supplies

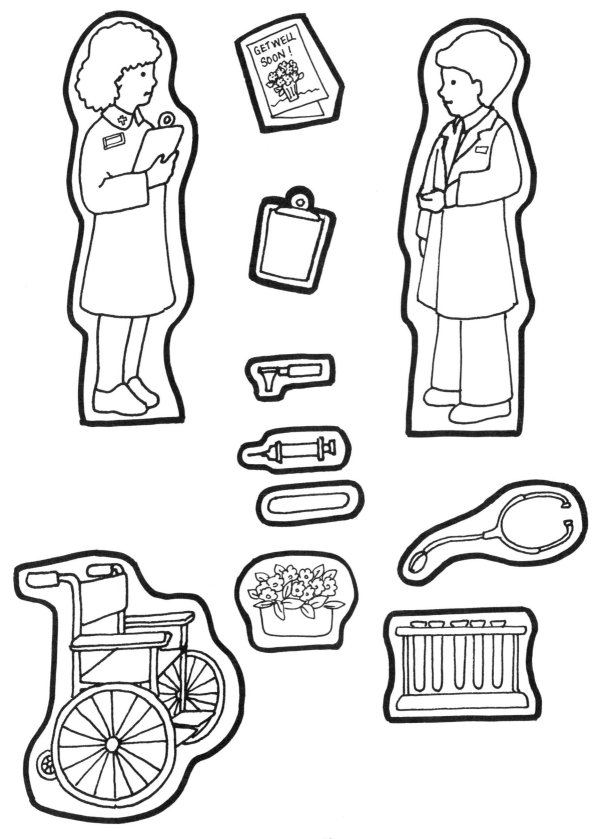

GET WELL SOON !

Around Town–Police Station

44

Around Town–Police Station
Police Station Employees and Supplies

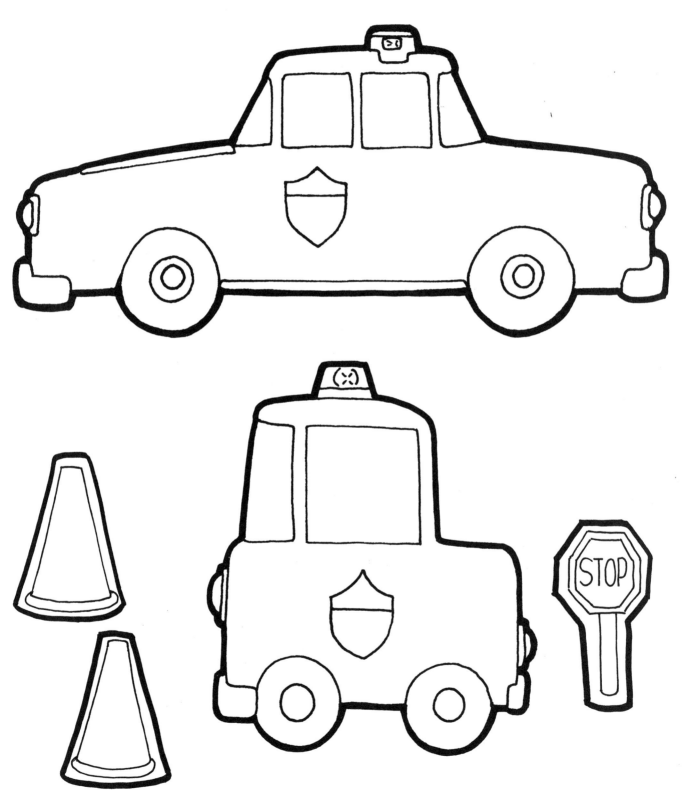

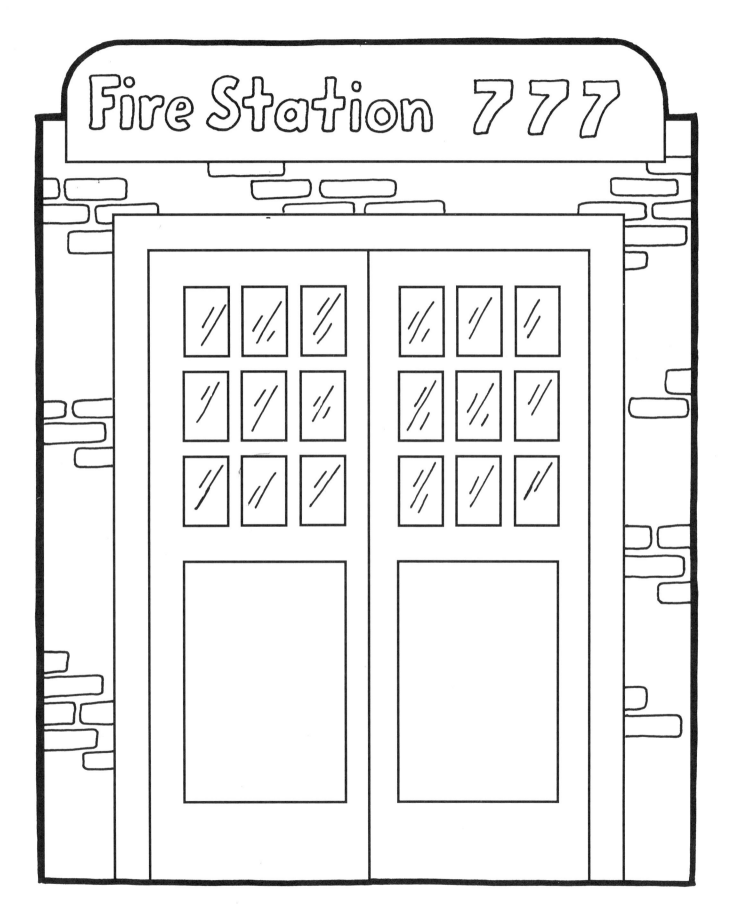

Fire Station 777

Around Town–Fire Station
Fire Station Employees and Supplies

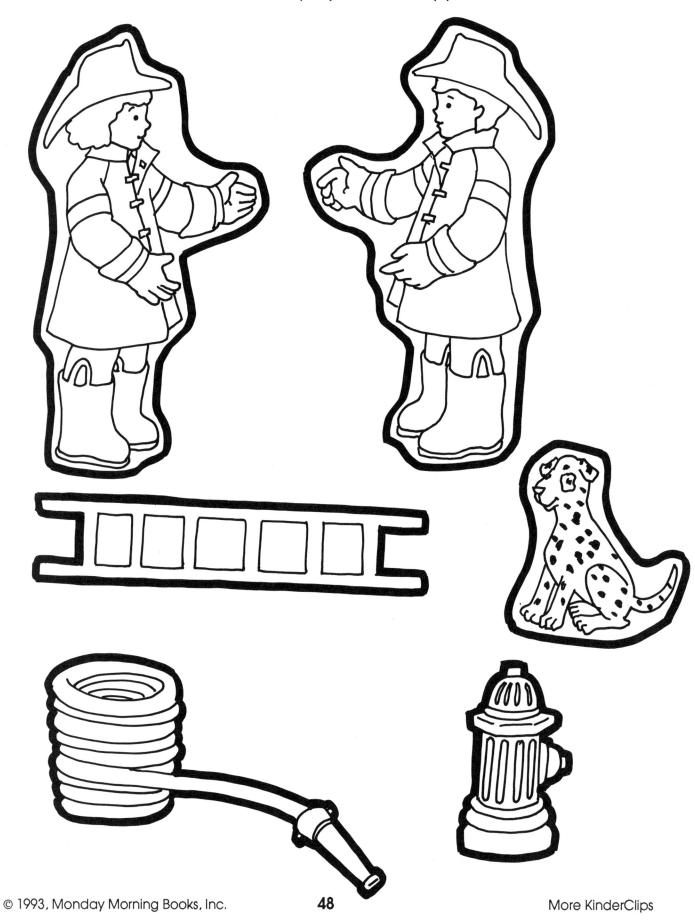

Around Town–Fire Station
Fire Engine

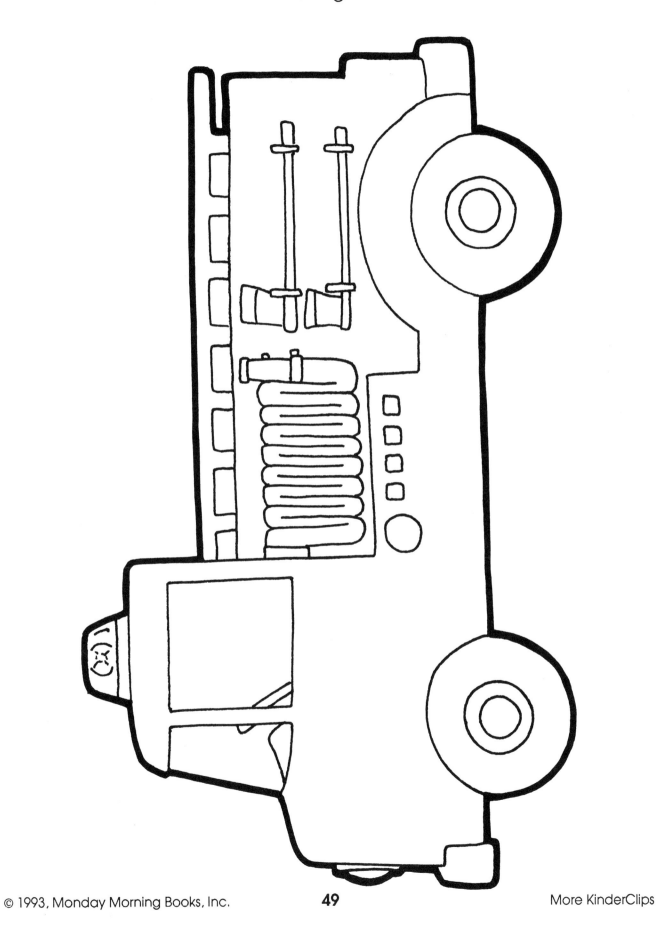

More KinderClips

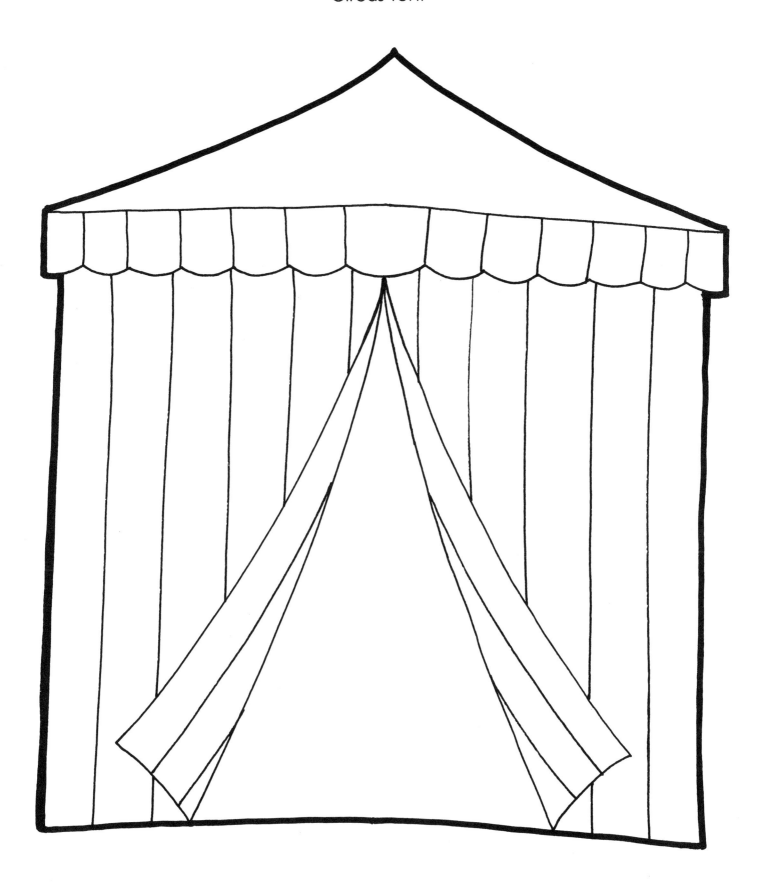

More KinderClips

Around Town–Circus
Circus Performers

Around Town–Circus
Circus Animals & Carousel

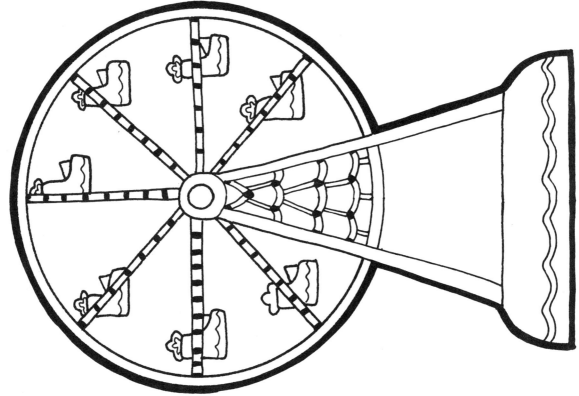

Around Town–Grocery Store
Grocery Store Employees & Shoppers

Around Town—Grocery Store
Fruit & Vegetables

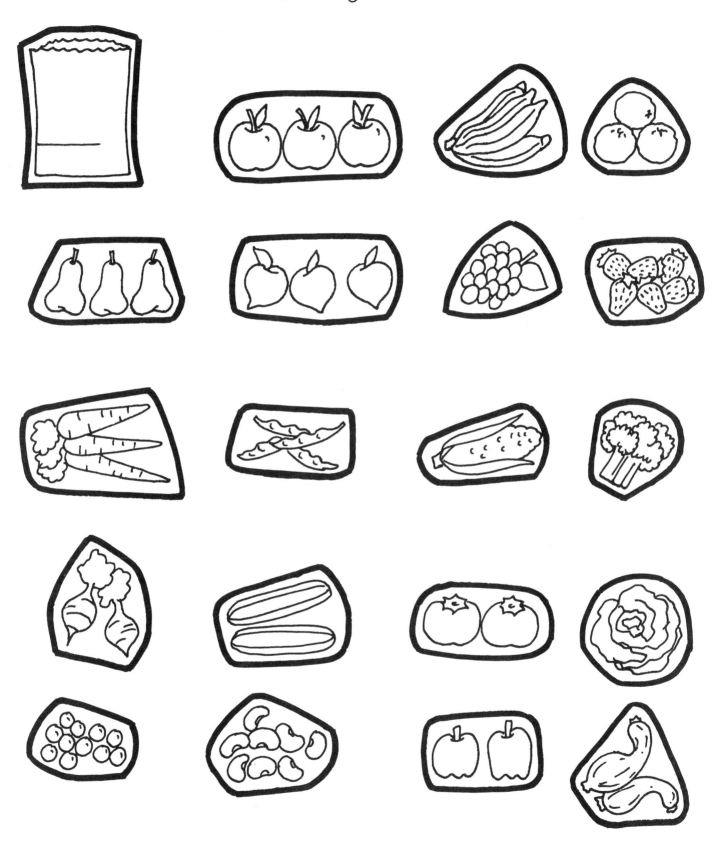

Around Town–Grocery Store
Packaged Food and Dry Goods

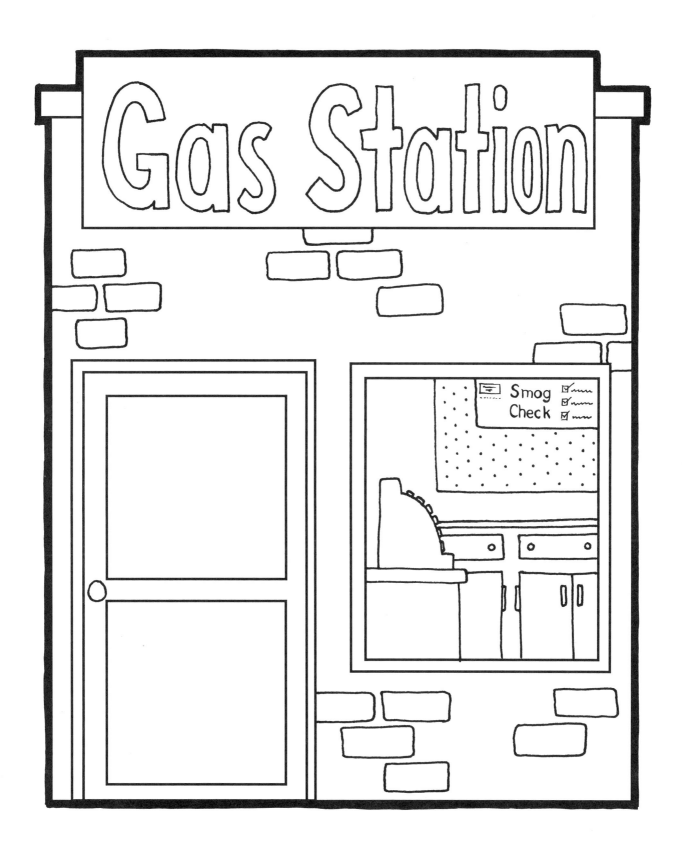

Around Town–Gas Station
Gas Station Attendant and Supplies

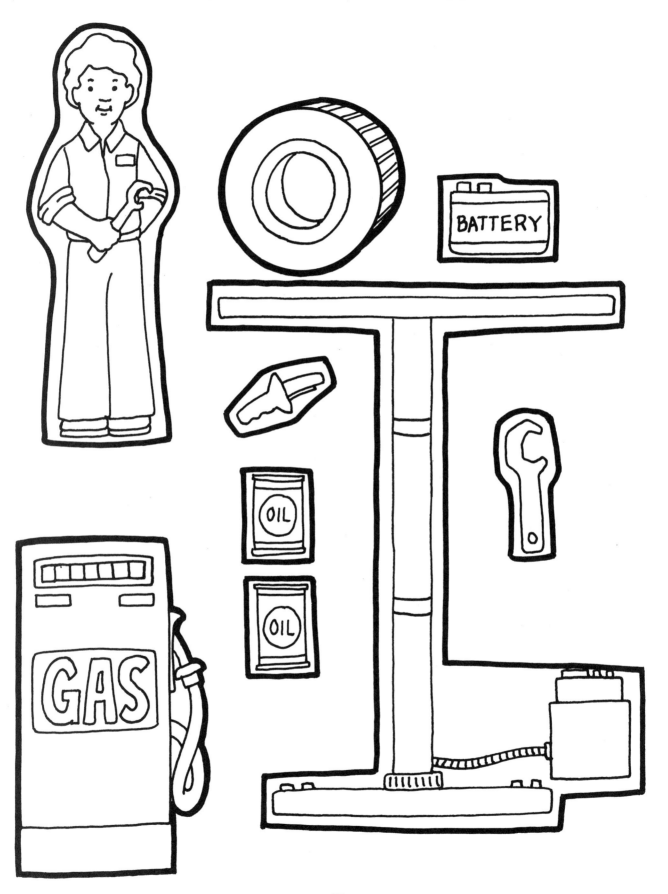

BATTERY

OIL

OIL

GAS

Around Town–Gas Station
Car

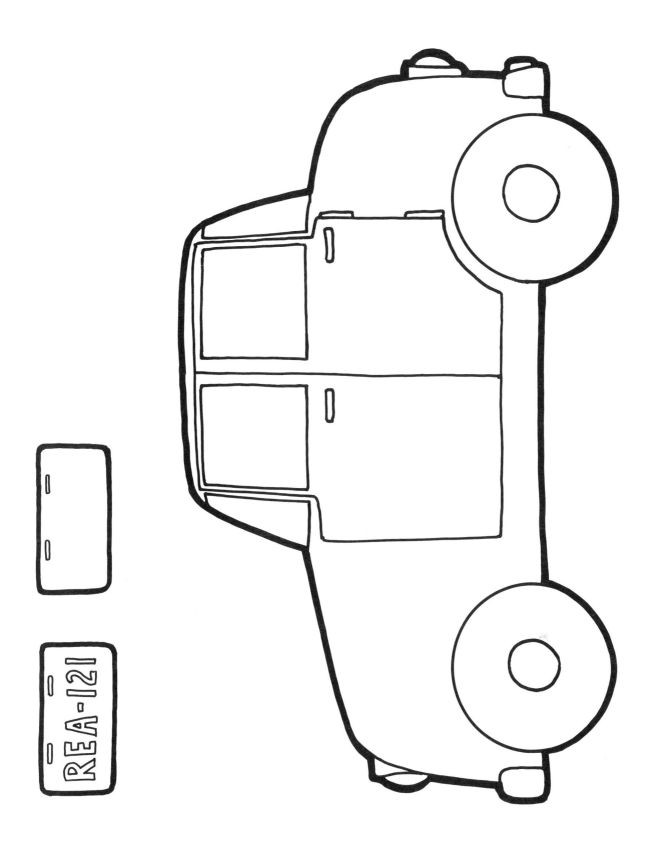

63

More KinderClips

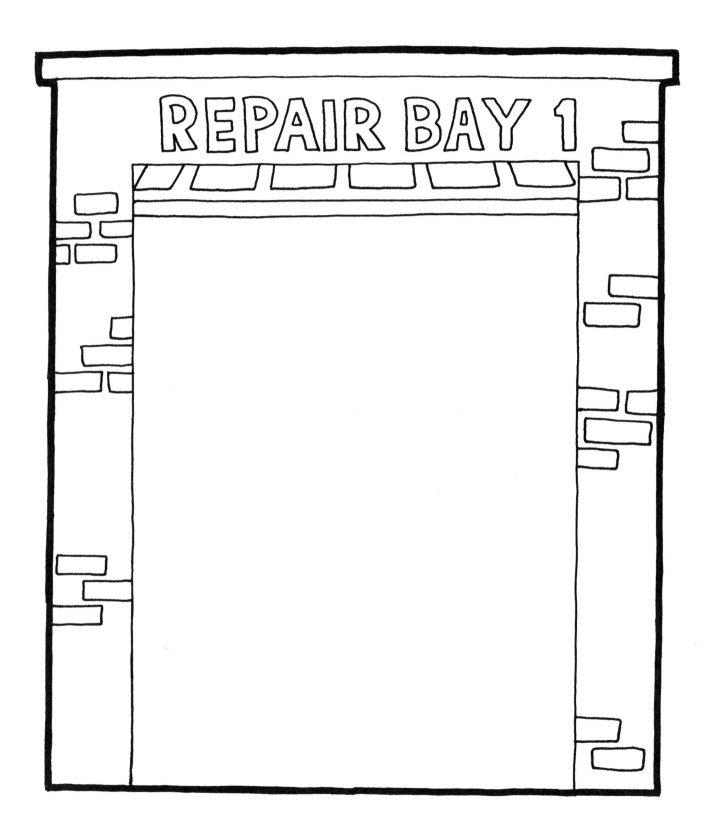

More KinderClips

Farm Family

More KinderClips

Around Town–Farm
Farm Equipment

67

Farm Animals

Around Town–Movie Theater
Theater Ushers and Supplies

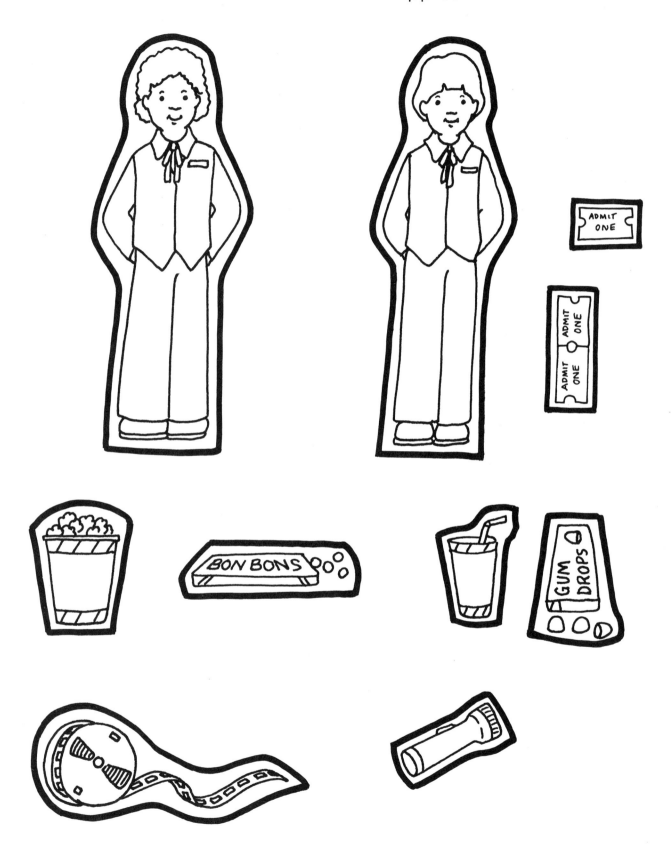

Around Town–Movie Theater
Theater Marquis and Letters

Around Town–Movie Theater
Movie Screen

 More KinderClips

Around Town–Restaurant
Restaurant Employees and Customers

Around Town–Restaurant
Restaurant Supplies

Around Town–Post Office

Around Town–Post Office
Mail Carriers and Supplies

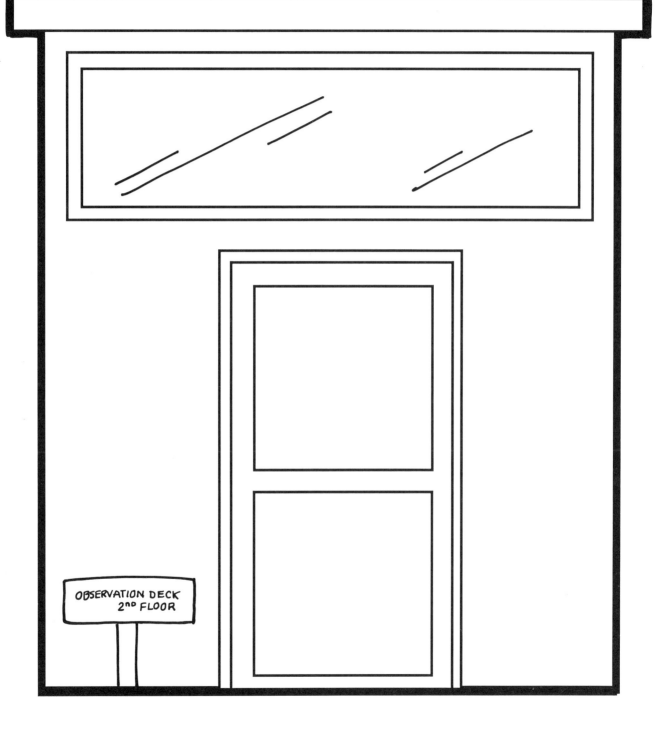

International Airport

OBSERVATION DECK
2ND FLOOR

Around Town–Airport
Airport Employees

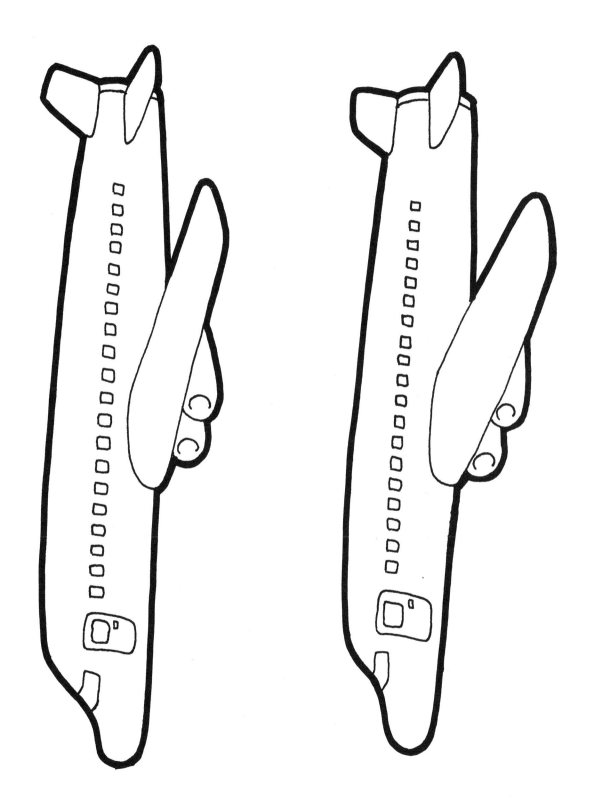

Around Town–Airport
Passengers and Supplies

More KinderClips

Around Town–Music Shop
Music Shop Employees

Around Town–Music Shop
Musical Instruments

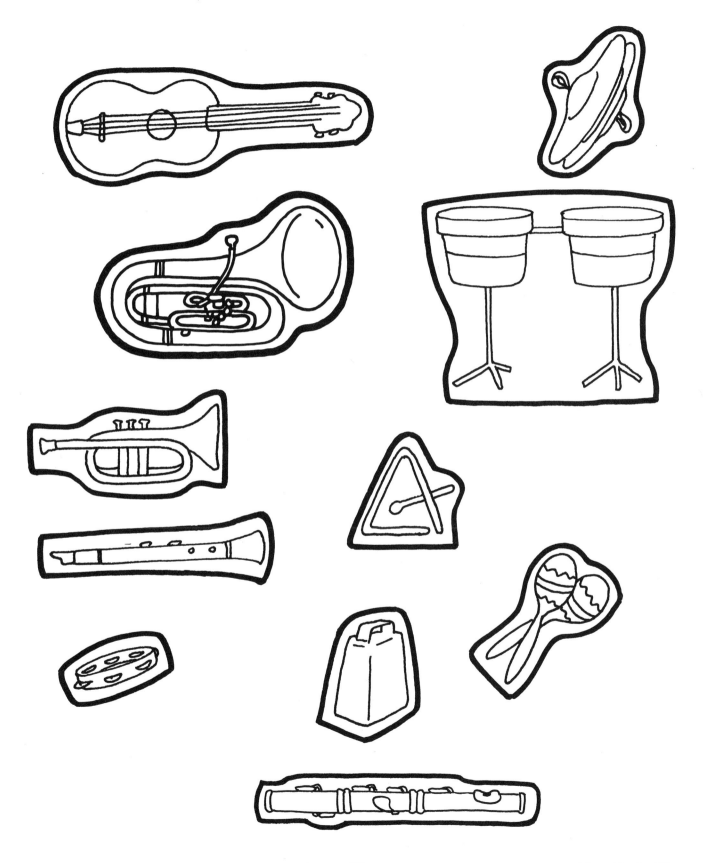

More KinderClips

Around Town–Props
Neighborhood Props, Signs, & Foliage

Around Town–Props
Neighborhood Vehicles

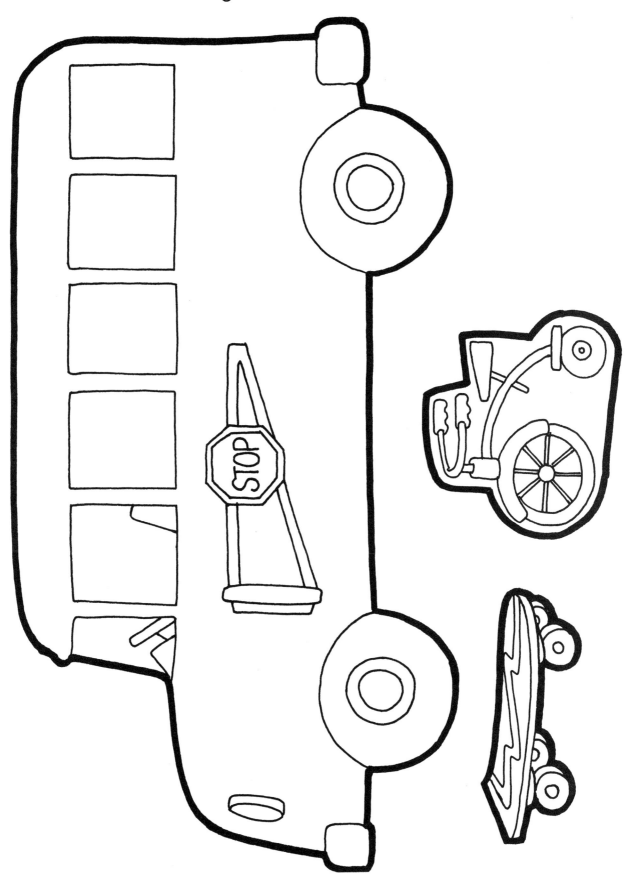

More KinderClips

89

Around Town–Props

Railroad Crossing & Train

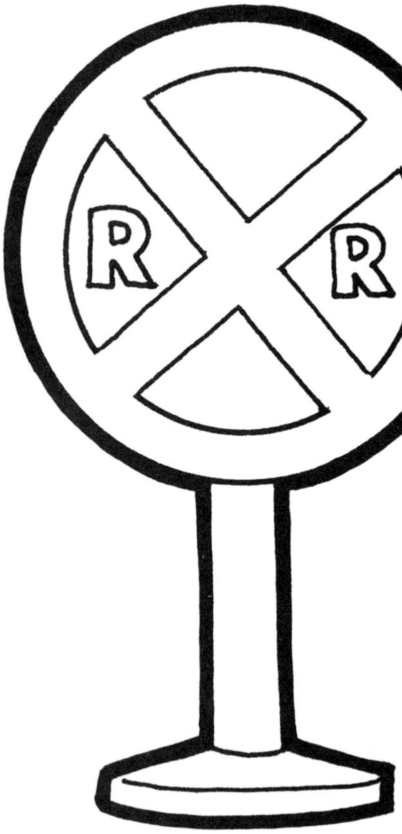

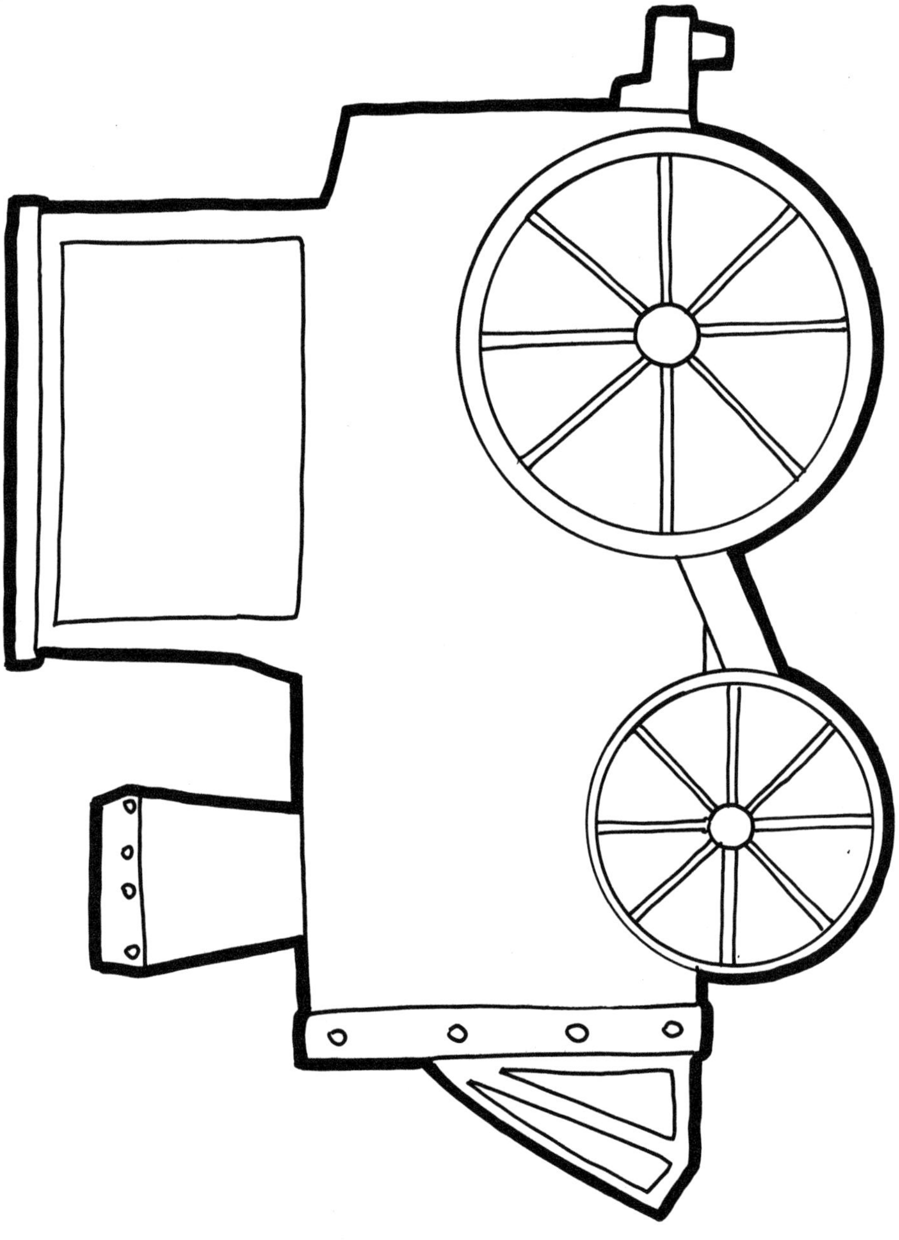

Around Town–Props
Bridge and Boats

More KinderClips

January

HAPPY NEW YEAR

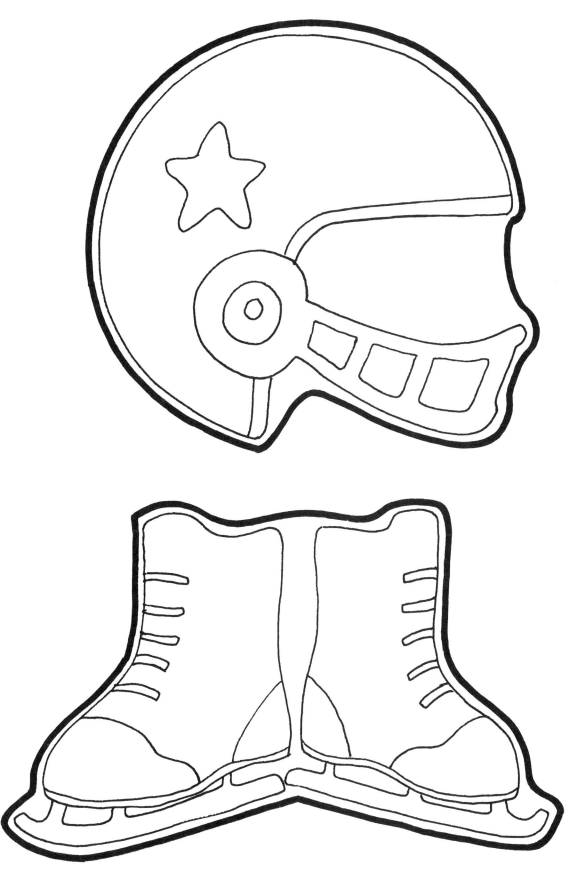

95

February

More KinderClips

NATIONAL BROTHERHOOD AND SISTERHOOD

NATIONAL BROTHERHOOD & SISTERHOOD WEEK

More KinderClips

March

NATIONAL
PEANUT
MONTH

Pig Month

YOUTH ART
MONTH

April

KEEP AMERICA BEAUTIFUL

HANS CHRISTIAN ANDERSEN

HAPPY BIRTHDAY

More KinderClips

More KinderClips

May

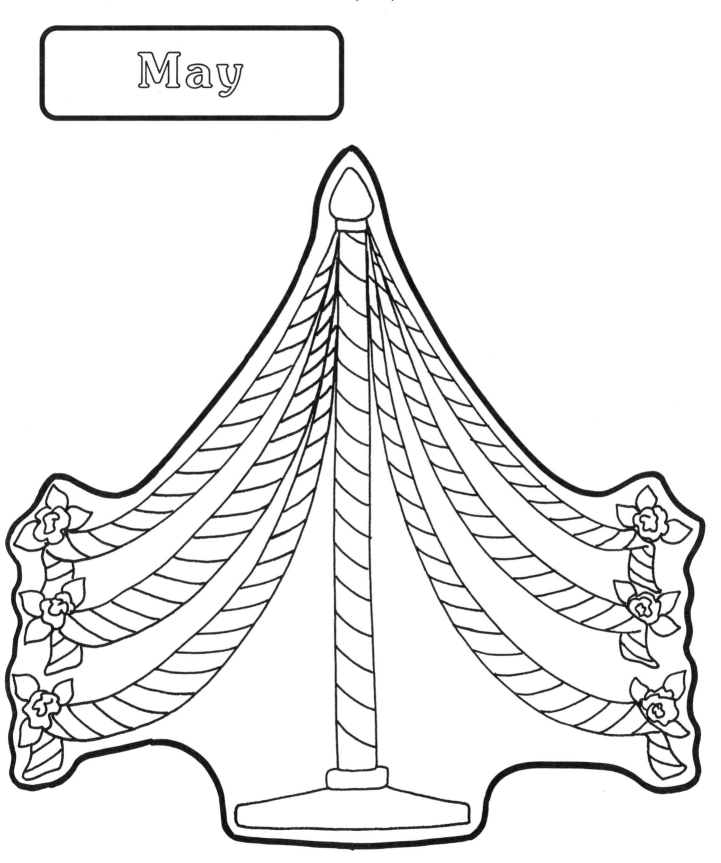

QUEEN FOR A DAY
Happy Mother's Day!

More KinderClips

June

110

More KinderClips

July

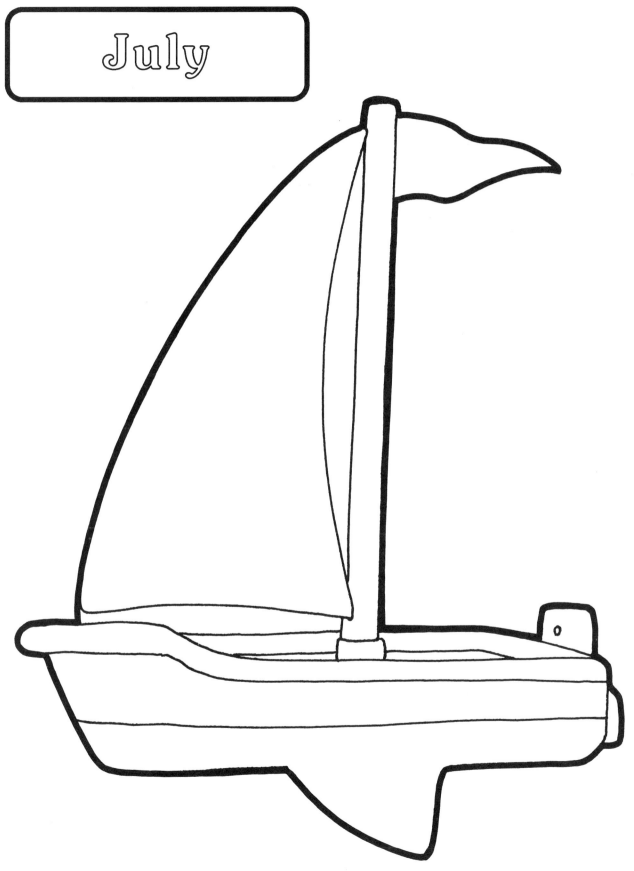

More KinderClips

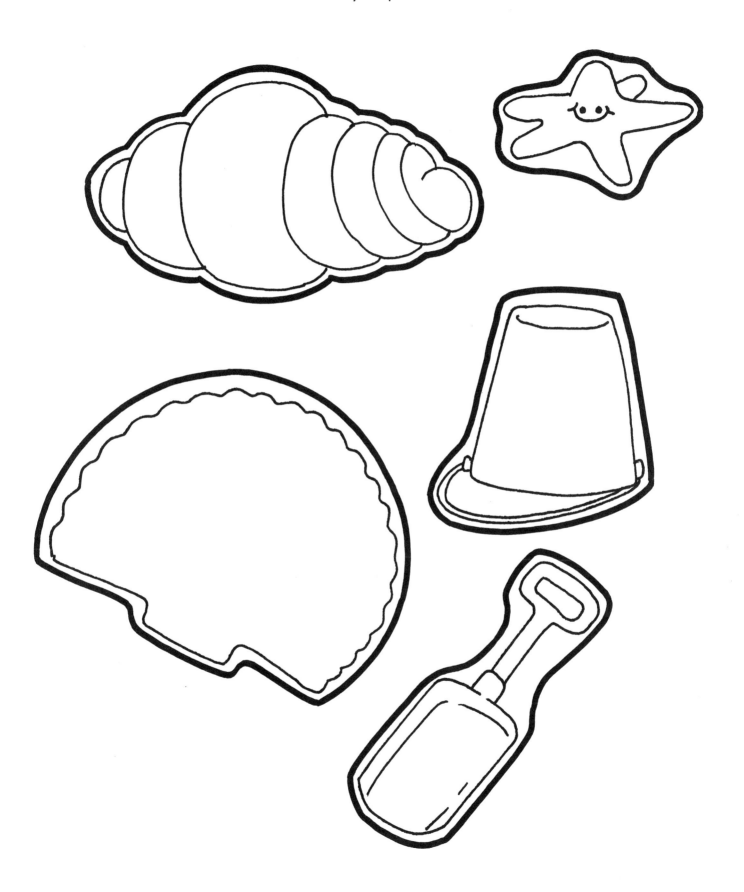

August

Throughout the Year
August Clips

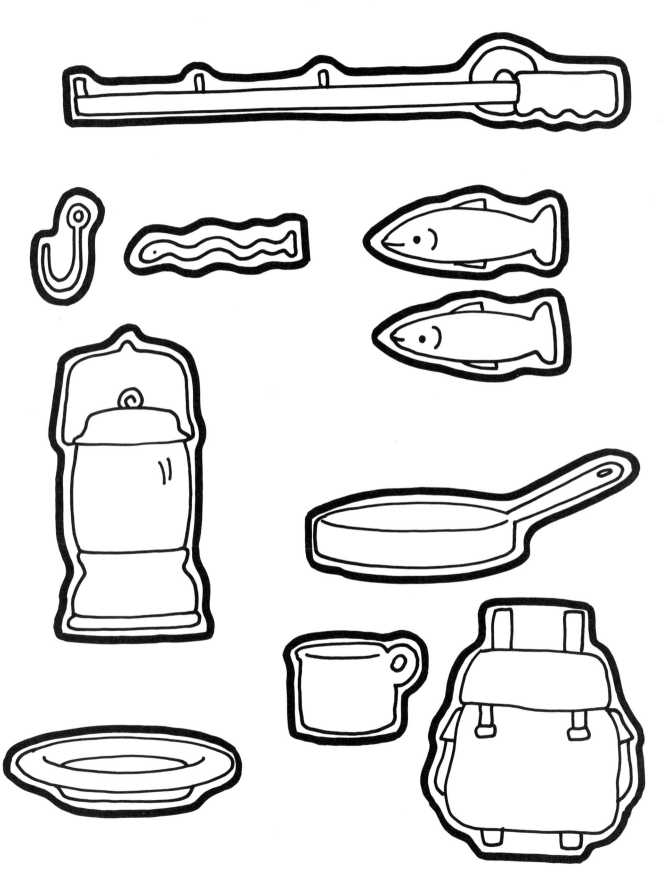

More KinderClips

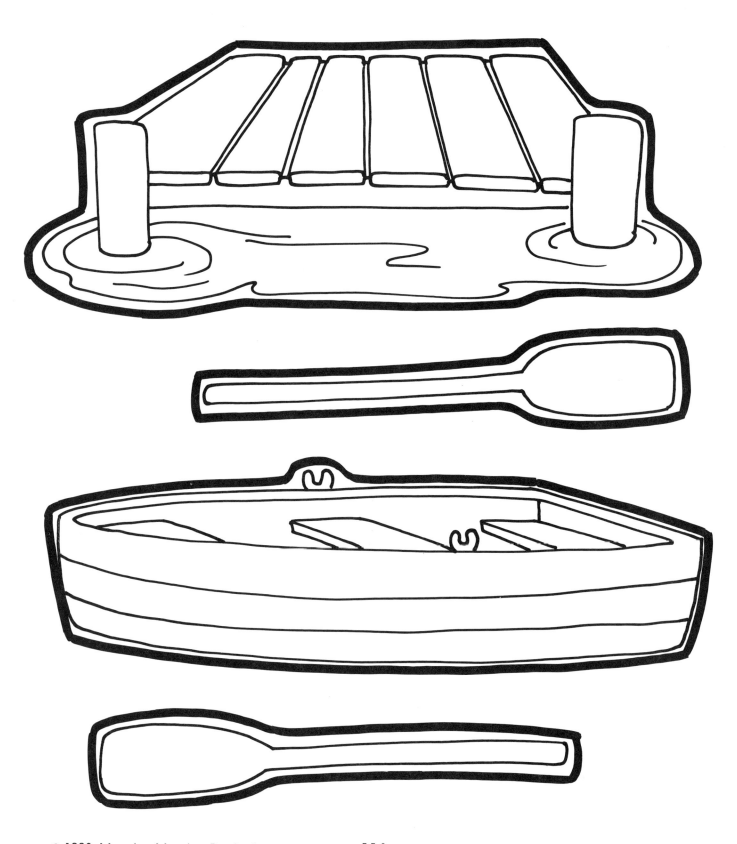

More KinderClips

September

JUICE

WELCOME
TO
MY CLASS!

October

November

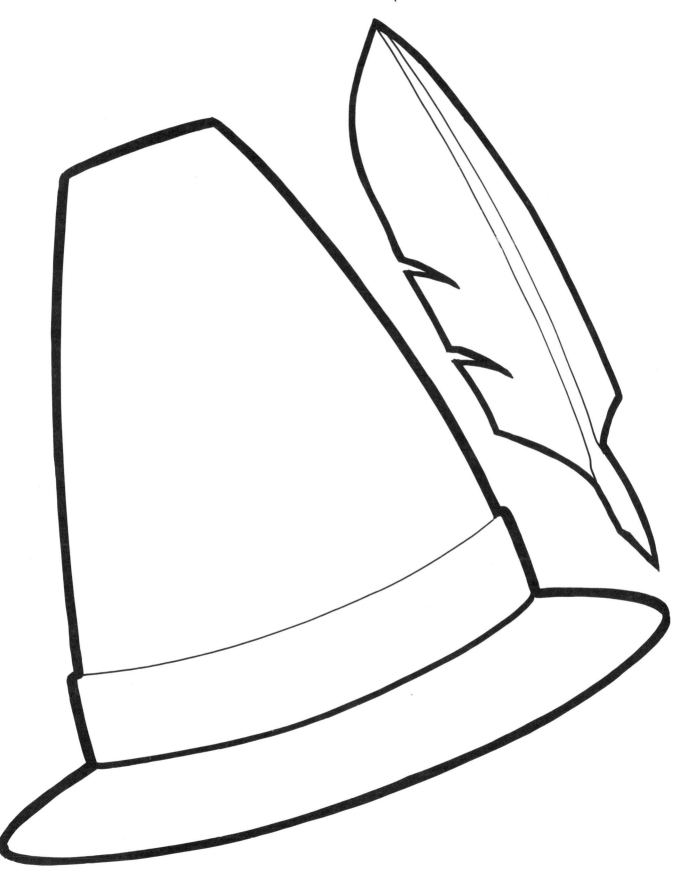

More KinderClips

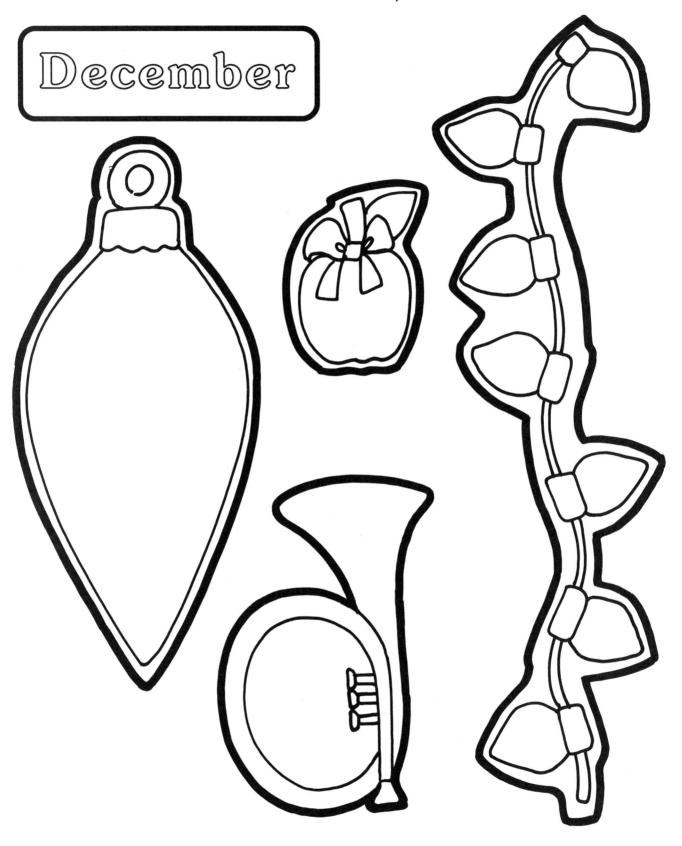

December

Throughout the Year

December Clips

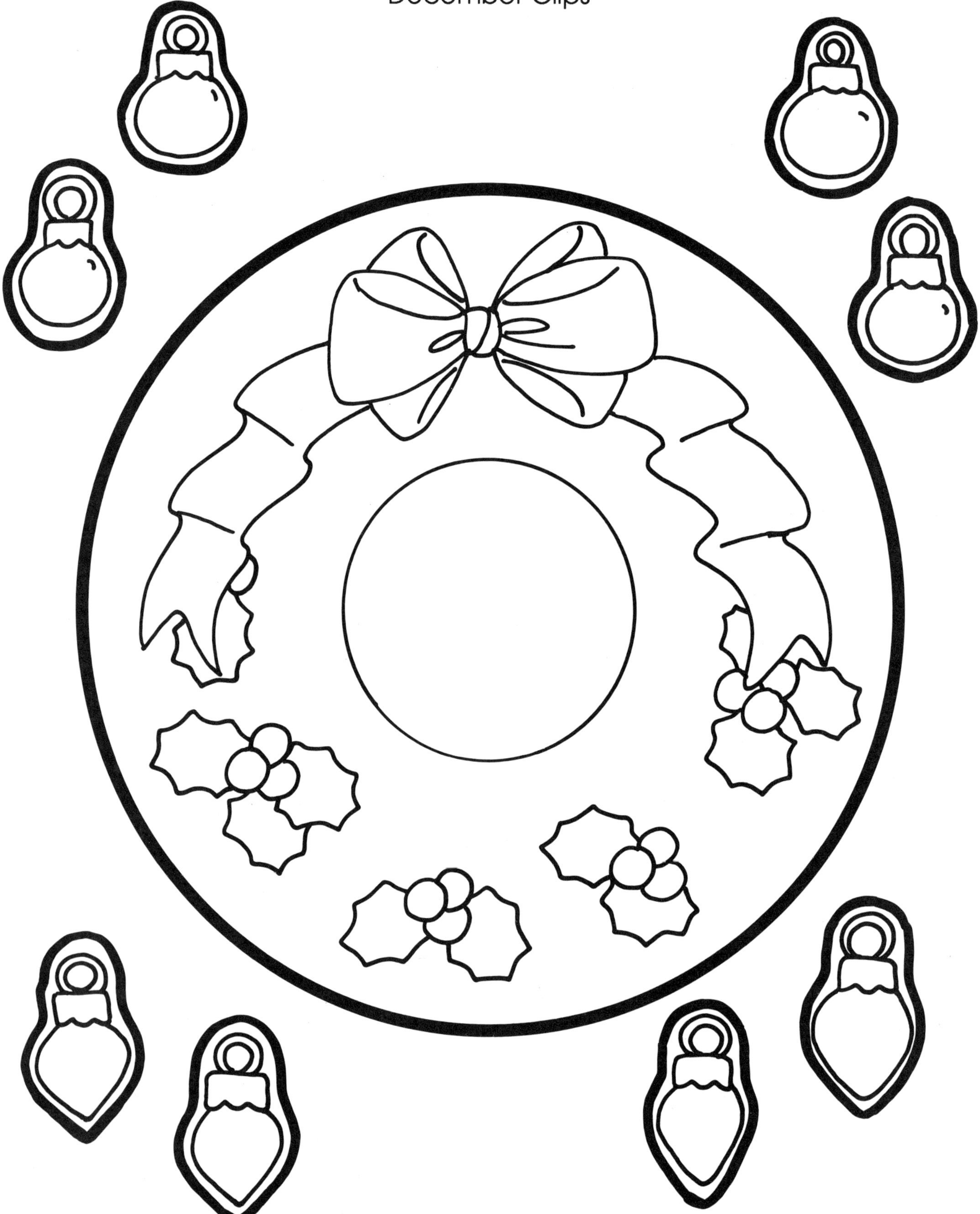